# As I Love

Written By
## Coleen Everglades Lewis

Illustrated By
## Bijan Samaddar

As I Love

Hardcover ISBN  978-1-7345570-3-9
Paperback ISBN 978-1-7345570-1-5
eBook ISBN 978-1-7345570-4-6

Written by Coleen Everglades Lewis

Illustrated by Bijan Samaddar

Patty Spoonbill
BOOKS

Thanks to my husband Ivan,
my sons, Jason, Brandon,
Ivan Jadon and my sister Debbie,
for their continued support.

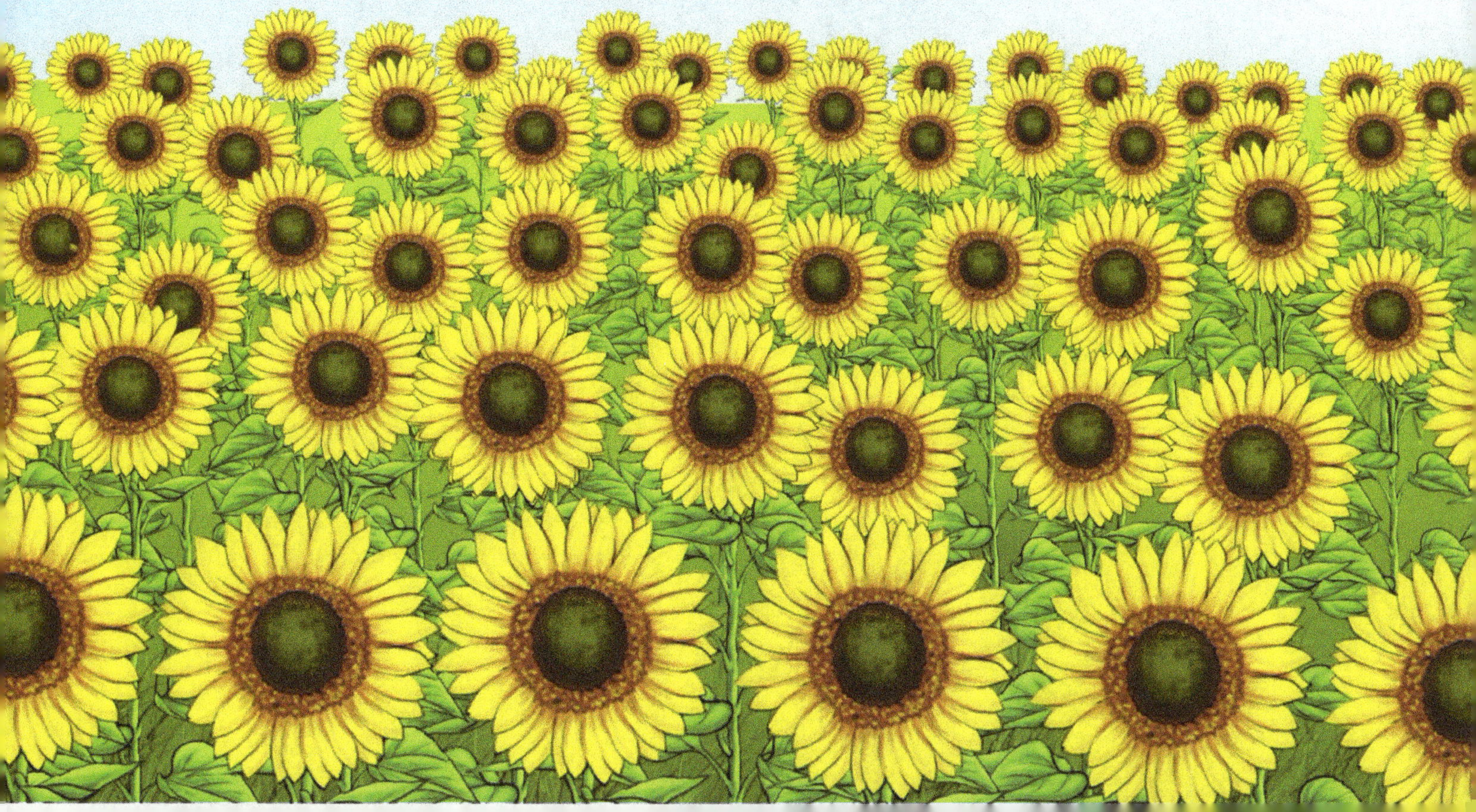

I am me,

a box of many colors.

# I am goofy.

# I am smart.

I am the color
outside the line.

Me,
I love me.

Happy me,
a bubble of laughter.

I am the sunrays
bouncing from the treetops.

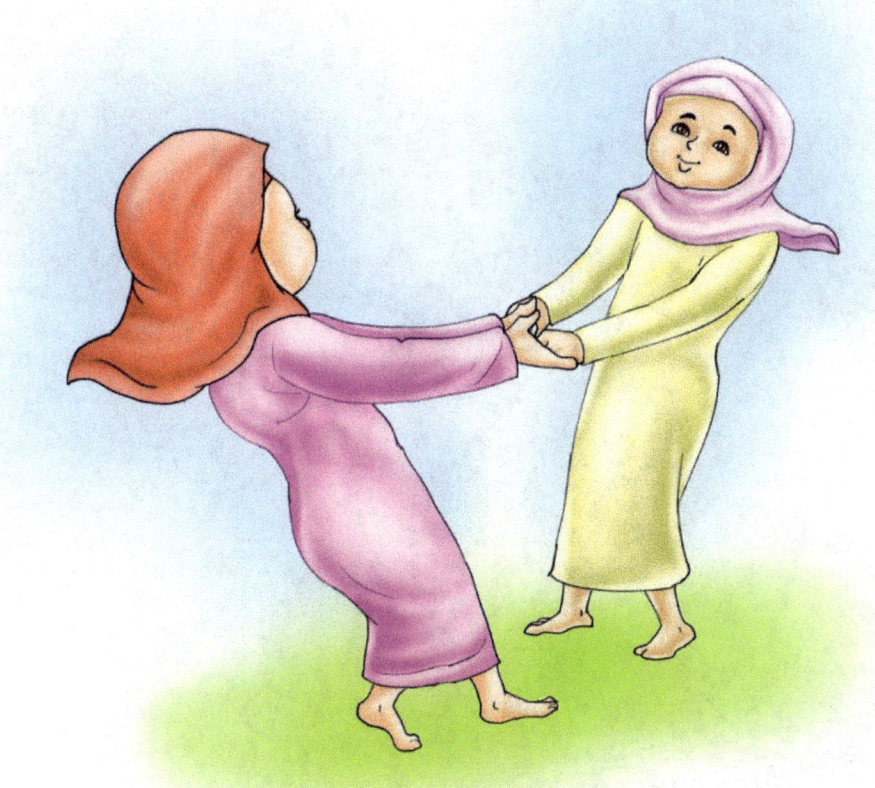

# I am the wildflower swaying in the soft breeze.

A paintbrush of
colors writes:
See me,
here I am.
I am here,
See me.

Me,
I love me.

As I cry, storm clouds burst into tears and rain on my face.

After the rain
comes sunshine.

My tears become a smile.

Strong me.

I love me.

I am free to love.
I love freely.

Me,
I love me.

the dreamer.

Children cannot fly like butterflies. Dreams can.

Starry-eyed me.

I love me.

I am one star in the galaxy.

I am one light among many lights.

When we shine together,
we become a galaxy of stars
that brighten our world.

Accepting me,
I love me.

And I love awesome you.

CPSIA information can be obtained
at www.ICGtesting.com
Printed in the USA
LVHW061441090420
652382LV00027B/476